Written originally at tl
one of the outstanding
at the end of the seventeenth century. Having survived some
thirty turbulent years of persecution, they needed some biblical
direction as to how to conduct their life together as gathered
churches. Benjamin Keach's book met this need. He was
concerned for the corporate life of the people of God, that they
understood who they were, how their life was to be ordered by
the word of Christ, and how they were to fulfill their
responsibilities as members of the church.

He emphasized the *glory* of the church—a much needed
emphasis in the early decades of the twenty-first century when
that glory has been so tarnished. Keach believed that God had
invested his glory into the churches of Christ and in their
authority and power. That glory derived from the head of the
body, the Lord Jesus Christ, and was to be displayed not only
in the way the church ordered its affairs, but also by the
holiness of each of the members, by their sincere love and
prayers for one another, and by their bearing with one
another's burdens and weaknesses.

Church discipline was to be put into practice when the
purity of the church was threatened by false teaching or
scandalous conduct among its members. This is a very
welcome addition to those works of Keach which are in the
process of being republished. Baptists today would do well to
consider carefully what Keach had to say and to assess whether
what he said is not as relevant today as it was in the 1690s.

—Austin Walker, a pastor of Maidenbower Baptist Church,
Crawley, UK, and author of *The Excellent Benjamin Keach*

Because of their historical context at the beginning of the Baptist movement, the seventeenth-century English Baptists thought deeply about the nature of the church. Their writings are an important corrective to the lackadaisical approach taken by many in our day. Benjamin Keach's *The Glory of a True Church* is the climax of the seventeenth-century Baptist literature on the church. It remains a faithful guide for pastors and churches to aid them in a recovering of a biblical understanding of the church.

—G. Stephen Weaver, Jr., PhD
Senior Pastor, Farmdale Baptist Church

The purpose, function, discipline, and problems of the local church have not changed since Benjamin Keach wrote this excellent work in the late seventeenth-century. That is why I love it so much and think it is such a valuable resource for Christians today. Keach believed that the church is beautiful, and that *church membership* is to be taken seriously. I agree! My prayer is that all true Christians will come to see the glory of a true church.

—Jeffrey D. Johnson, D.Min
Author of *The Church: Why Bother?*

Without question, Benjamin Keach was the greatest theologian among Baptists of the second-generation. He was also a faithful pastor who cared deeply for the church, and longed to see it ordered according to God's revealed will. In this little tract, *The Glory of a True Church*, Keach brilliantly, clearly, and succinctly explains the nature of church polity as well as regular and orderly church discipline. I highly recommend it to scholars, pastors, and laymen alike!

—Tom Hicks, PhD
A pastor of Morningview Baptist Church

THE GLORY

OF A

TRUE CHURCH

BENJAMIN KEACH

THE GLORY

OF A

TRUE CHURCH

BENJAMIN KEACH

1697

FREE GRACE PRESS

The Glory of a True Church

Benjamin Keach

Originally title: The Glory of a True Church, And its Discipline displayed Wherein a true Gospel-Church is described. Together with the power of the Keys, and who are to be let in, and who to be shut out.

Originally published in 1697
by John Robinson, London

Reprinted and updated by
      Free Grace Press, 2015
      1455 Champions Rd.
      Conway, AR 72034

Cover design by Scott Schaller

Printed in the United States of America

Contents

Foreword

Benjamin Keach was born in Stokeham, England, Feb. 29, 1640. He found peace through Christ in his fifteenth year; and being unable to discover infant baptism or baptism by sprinkling in the Bible, and being fully satisfied that every believer should be immersed, he was baptized after the Savior's example by John Russel, and united with a neighboring Baptist church. This community, perceiving his remarkable talents, encouraged him, when he was eighteen years old, to exercise his gifts as a minister.

At first he was an Arminian about the extent of the atonement and free-will, but the reading of the Scriptures and the conversation of those who knew the will of God more perfectly relieved him from both errors. In 1668, in the twenty-eighth year of his age, he was ordained pastor of the church of Horsleydown, Southwark, London.

The congregation increased so rapidly after Mr. Keach became pastor, that they had to repeatedly enlarge their house of worship.

Mr. Keach soon became a famous disputant on the Baptist side; he had taken Richard Baxter in hand, the serious injury of the Bishop of Kidderminster, and others felt his heavy blows.

The Rev. John Tredwell of Lavingham, a friend of Mr. Keach, was blessed in his ministry by the conversion of several vicious persons, who united with his church; this stirred up the indignation of the Rev. Wm. Burkitt, the commentator, a neighbor of Mr. Tredwell, who cast many unjust reflections upon the Baptists and their doctrines. Mr. Tredwell wrote Mr. Burkitt giving some reasons why he should abandon the unchristian course he was pursuing. Mr. Burkitt, at a time when Mr. Tredwell and his people were gathered in the sanctuary for public worship, with a number of his parishioners, entered the meeting-house, and demanded that Mr. Tredwell and his church should hear his view of the points in dispute. Mr. Tredwell, taken aback somewhat by "such a riotous and tumultuous challenge," agreed to let him speak against Baptist beliefs and usages, provided that he should have an opportunity to reply. For nearly two hours Mr. Burkitt sustained infant baptism, and then he and his riotous company departed without giving Mr. Tredwell an opportunity of making any return, except to a few of his own persuasion that were left behind. Mr. Burkitt speedily published the substance of the address that so rudely intruded upon the Baptist minister and his people. Mr. Keach, as a valiant defender of the faith, was invited to reply to Mr. Burkitt's arguments, which he did effectively in "The Rector Rectified and Corrected." Mr. Burkitt was rector of Dedham.

He was challenged by some Episcopal ministers to discuss baptism at Gravesend, near London. As he went to that place in a boat with some friends, he incidentally alluded to the proposed meeting in a way that permitted a stranger, an Episcopal minister, to know that he was Mr. Keach. This person attacked him about infant baptism, and received such a complete drubbing that as soon as the boat touched land he started for his Episcopal brethren and informed them of the arguments which Mr. Keach would use and of his method of putting them. The result of the interview between Mr. Keach's fellow-traveler in the Gravesend boat and his brethren was that they went away as quickly as possible, leaving Mr. Keach without an antagonist.

Mr. Keach was often in prison for preaching, and his life was frequently in danger. Some cavalry sent down to Buckinghamshire to suppress the religious meetings of dissenters found Mr. Keach preaching, and swore that they would kill him. He was seized and bound and laid on the earth and four of the troopers were ready to trample him to death with their horses; but just as they were going to put spurs to their horses an officer who perceived their object rode up and stopped them. He was taken to prison, from which he obtained a release after suffering great hardships.

In 1664, he wrote *The Child's Instructor*. For the heresies against the Episcopal Church in the little work, he was arrested and bound over under heavy penalties to appear at court. The assizes began at Aylesbury Oct. 8, 1664. The judge was Lord Chief Justice Hyde, afterwards Lord Clarendon, who acted like Jeffreys at the "Bloody Assizes." Lord Clarendon abused Mr. Keach outrageously, as he threatened the jury and evidently wanted to have Mr. Keach executed if he could terrify him into making some unwise statements.

The jury brought in a verdict that Mr. Keach was guilty in part. And when asked to explain their verdict, the foreman said, "In the indictment he is charged with these words, 'When the thousand years shall be expired, then shall all the rest of the devils be raised'; but in the book it is, 'Then shall the rest of the dead be raised.'"

The judge informed the jury that they could bring him in guilty of all the indictments but that sentence. They brought in the prompted verdict. And immediately the judge said: "Benjamin Keach, you are here convicted for writing, printing, and publishing a seditious and schismatical book, for which the court's judgment is that you go to jail for a fortnight without bail, and the next Saturday stand upon the pillory at Aylesbury in the open market for the space of two hours, with a paper upon your head with this inscription, 'For writing, printing, and publishing a schismatical book entitled "The Child's Instructor, or a New and Easy Primer,"' and the next Thursday to stand in the same manner and for the same time in the market of Winslow; and then your book shall be openly burnt before your face by the common hangman in disgrace of you and your doctrine. And you shall forfeit to the king's majesty the sum of twenty pounds; and shall remain in jail until you find sureties for your good behavior and appearance at the next assizes, there to renounce your doctrines and make such public submission as shall be enjoined upon you." The sheriff was as rigorous in executing this infamous sentence as the judge was insolent in pronouncing it.

On the pillory at Aylesbury Mr. Keach defended himself and the truth with great boldness. The jailer frequently interrupted him, and finally, the sheriff himself threatened to have him gagged. The people, contrary to custom, had no words of mockery for the good, persecuted minister, and no offensive missile was hurled at him.

An Episcopal minister who ventured to assail Mr. Keach in the pillory was immediately reproached by the people with the ungodliness of his own life, and his voice was drowned in laughter. At Winslow, where he lived, he suffered the same shameful penalty, and a copy of his little book was burned.

Mr. Keach was a zealous Baptist. He aided ministers who came to him from all parts of his country, and he had many meeting-houses built. His works in defense of Baptist principles were read all over the kingdom. Before his death, men spoke of him as the "famous" Mr. Keach, and he is still described by writers as a man of great celebrity. His two most popular works are *Tropologia*, or *A Key to Open Scripture Metaphors*, and *Gospel Mysteries Unveiled*, or *An Exposition of All the Parables*.

The latter work, *An Exposition of All the Parables*, is more frequently offered for sale in the catalogues of the great London second-hand bookstores than any production of Richard Baxter, John Howe, or Jeremy Taylor.

Mr. Keach was the author of forty-three works. He died July 18, 1704, in his sixty-fourth year. He was a devout Christian who led a blameless life and died in the triumphs of faith.

—William Cathcart, 1881

Introduction

To the baptized churches, particularly to that under my care.

My brethren, every house or building consists of both matter and form: and so does the church of Christ, or house of the living God.

The matter or materials with which it is built are lively stones (i.e., converted persons). Also, the matter and form must be according to the rule and pattern shown in the mount (I mean Christ's institution, and the apostolical church's constitution), and not after men's inventions.

Now some men, because the typical church of the Jews was national, and took in their carnal seed (as such); therefore, the same matter and form they would have under the Gospel.

But though a church is rightly built in both these respects (i.e., of fit matter and right form), without a regular and orderly discipline, it will soon lose its beauty—as it will be polluted.

Many reverend divines of the congregational way have written most excellently (it is true) upon this subject, I mean on church-discipline. But, the books are so voluminous that the poorer sort can't purchase them, and many others have not time or learning enough to improve them to their profit; and our brethren the Baptists have not written (as I can gather) on this subject by itself.

Therefore, I have been earnestly desired by our members and by one of our pastors to write a small and plain tract concerning the rules of the discipline of a gospel church; that all men may not only know our faith, but see our order in this case also. True, this, though plain, is but short, but maybe it will provoke some other person to do it more fully. Certainly, ignorance of the rules of discipline causes no small trouble and disorders in our churches; and if this may be a prevention, or prove profitable to any, let God have the glory, and I have my end: who am yours

—Benjamin Keach

1
The Order of the Church

Before there can be any orderly discipline among a Christian assembly, they must be orderly and regularly constituted into a church-state: according to the institution of Christ in the gospel.

A True Church Defined

A church of Christ is a congregation of godly Christians, who as a stated assembly (being first baptized upon the profession of faith) do by mutual agreement and consent give themselves up to the Lord, and one to another, according to the will of God; and do ordinarily meet together in one place, for the public service and worship of God; among whom the word of God and sacraments are duly administered, according to Christ's institution.[1]

---

[1] Acts 2:41-44, Acts 8:14, Acts 19:4-6, Eph. 1:1-2, 2:12-13, 19, Col. 1:2-4, 12, 1 Pet. 2:5, Acts 5:13-14, Rom. 6:17, Heb. 6:1-2

The Beauty of a True Church

The beauty and glory of which congregation does consist in their being all converted persons, or *lively stones*; being by the Holy Spirit united to Jesus Christ, the precious corner-stone and only foundation of every Christian, as well as of every particular congregation, and of the whole *catholic church*.[2]

Requirement for Church Membership

That every person before they are admitted as members, in such a church so constituted, must declare to the church (or to such with the pastor, that they shall appoint) what God has done for their souls, or their experiences of a saving work of grace upon their hearts. Moreover, the church should enquire after and take full satisfaction concerning their holy lives, or good conversations.[3]

Responsibilities of Church Membership

When admitted into membership, they must solemnly enter into a covenant before the church to walk in the fellowship of that particular congregation. They must

[2] Rom. 6:3-5, 1 Pet. 2:4-6, Eph. 2:20-21, Col. 2:19
[3] Ps. 66:16, Acts 11:4-6, &c., 23-24. 1 Pet. 3:15, 2 Cor. 8:5, Jer. 50:5

submit themselves to the care and discipline thereof[4] and to walk faithfully with God in all his holy ordinances. They agree to be fed, have communion, and worship God there, when the church meets (if possible); and give themselves up to the watch and charge of the pastor and ministry thereof.[5]

The pastor then, signifying in the name of the church their acceptance of each person, and endeavors to take the care of them, and to watch over them in the Lord (the members being first satisfied to receive them and to have communion with them). And so, the pastor is to give them the right hand of fellowship of a church, or church *organic*.

A church thus constituted ought forthwith to choose them a pastor—elder or elders—and deacons (we reading of no other officers or offices abiding in the church). And, what kind of men they ought to be, and how qualified, is laid down by *Paul* to *Timothy* and to *Titus*.

Moreover, they are to take special care that bishops, overseers, or elders, as well as the deacons, have in some competent manner all those qualifications; and after in a day of solemn prayer and fasting, that they have elected

[4] Heb. 13:17
[5] 1 Pet. 5:1-2

them, (whether pastor, etc., or deacons) and they accepting the office, must be ordained with prayer, and laying on of hands of the eldership; being first proved, and found meet and fit persons for so sacred an office. Therefore, such are very disorderly churches who have no pastor or pastors ordained; they acting not according to the rule of the gospel, having something wanting.[6]

The Work of a Pastor

The work of a pastor is to preach the word of Christ, or to feed the flock, and to administer all the ordinances of the gospel which belong to his sacred office;[7] and to be faithful and laborious therein: "studying to show himself approved unto God, a workman that needs not be ashamed, rightly dividing the word of truth."[8]

Because he is a steward of the mysteries of God,[9] he ought to be a man of good understanding and experience, being sound in the faith, and one that is acquainted with the mysteries of the gospel: "Because he is to feed the

[6] 1 Tim. 3.2-7, Tit. 1:5-10, Tit. 1:7, Acts 6:6, 1 Tim. 5:22, 1 Cor. 9:16-17
[7] Acts 20:31, 35
[8] 2 Tim. 2:15, 2 Cor. 4:1-2, 1 Tim. 3
[9] 2 Cor. 4:1-2, 1 Tim. 3

people with knowledge and understanding."[10] He must be faithful and skillful to declare the mind of God, and diligent therein: also to "preach in season and out of season;"[11] God having committed unto him the ministry of reconciliation,[12] a most choice and sacred trust.

1. What greater interest in the world has God given to men than this? Moreover, he must make known the whole counsel of God to the people.[13]

2. A pastor is to visit his flock, to know "their state, and to watch over them, to support the weak, and to strengthen the feeble-minded,"[14] and succor the tempted, and to reprove them that are unruly.

3. He is to pray for his flock at all times, and with them also when sent for and desired, and as opportunity serves. He is to sympathize with them in every state and condition, with all love and compassion.

4. He is to show them in all respects, as near as he can, a good example in "conversation, charity, faith, and

[10] Jer. 3:15
[11] 2 Tim. 4:2
[12] 2 Cor. 5:19
[13] Acts 20:20, 27
[14] Pr. 27:23, 1 Thess. 5

purity."[15] He must be above reproach that his ministry may be the more acceptable to all, and the name of God be glorified, and religion be delivered from reproach.

5. He must see that he carries the truth to all with all impartiality, not preferring the rich above the poor, nor lord it over God's heritage, nor assume any greater power than God has given him; but to show a humble and meek spirit, nay to be *clothed with humility.*[16]

The Office and Work of Deacons

The work of deacons is to serve tables,[17] viz. to seek to provide for the Lord's Table, the minister's table, and the poor's table.[18]

1. They should provide bread and wine for the Lord's Table.

2. They should see that every member contributes to the maintenance of the ministry, according to their ability, and their own voluntary subscription or obligation.[19]

---

[15] 1 Tim. 4:12
[16] Jam. 2:4, 1 Tim. 5:21, 1 Pet. 5:3, 5:6
[17] Acts 6.1-3, 5, 7-10
[18] Acts 5:7-10
[19] 1 Cor. 16:2

3. They should see that each member do give weekly to the poor, as God has blessed him.

4. Also, they are to visit the poor, and know their condition as much as in them lies: that none, especially the aged widows, be neglected.[20]

Duties of Church Members to Their Pastor

1. It is the duty of members to pray for their pastor and teachers. *Brethren, pray for us,* that the Word of the Lord may run *and be glorified.*[21] Again, Paul said, "Praying also for us, that God would open unto us a door of utterance, to speak the mystery of Christ."[22] Prayer was made without ceasing by the church unto God for him. They that neglect this duty seem not to care either for their minister, or their own souls: or whether sinners be converted, and the church edified or not. They pray for their own daily bread, and will they not pray to have the Bread of Life plentifully broken to them?

Motives to this: (1.) A minister's work is great: "Who is sufficient for these things?"[23] (2.) The opposition is not

[20] Acts 6:1
[21] 1 Thess. 5:25
[22] Heb. 13:18
[23] 2 Cor. 2:16

small which is made against them.[24] (3.) God's loud call is (as well as ministers themselves) for the saint's continual prayer and supplication for them.[25] (4.) Their weaknesses and temptations are many. (5.) The increase and edification of the church depends upon the success of their ministry. (6.) If they fall or miscarry, God is greatly dishonored and his ways and people are reproached.

2. They ought to show a reverential estimation of them,[26] being Christ's ambassadors, also called rulers, angels, etc. they that honor and receive them, honor and receive Jesus Christ. "Esteem them very highly in love for their work's sake."[27] Again, he said, "let the elders that rule well, be accounted worthy of double honor, especially they who labor in word and doctrine." [28] That is, as I conceive, such that are most laborious.

3. It is their duty to submit themselves unto them, that is, in all their exhortations, good counsels, and reproofs; and when they call to any extraordinary duty, as prayer, fasting, or days of thanksgiving: if they see no just cause why such days should not be kept, they ought to obey

[24] 1 Cor. 16:9
[25] 1 Tim. 4:3-5
[26] 2 Cor. 3:19-20
[27] 1 Thess. 3:13
[28] 1 Tim. 5:17

their pastor or elder, as in other cases also. "Obey them that have the rule over you, and submit yourselves."[29]

4. It is their duty to take care to vindicate them from the unjust charges of evil men, or tongue of infamy, and not to take up a reproach against them by report; nor to grieve their spirits, or weaken their hands.[30]

5. It is the duty of members to go to them when under trouble or temptations.

6. It is their duty to provide a comfortable maintenance for them and their families, suitable to their state and condition. "Let him that is taught in the Word, communicate to him that teaches, in all good things."[31] Who goes to war at his own expense? Who plants a vineyard, and does not eat of the fruit thereof?[32] Even so has the Lord ordained that they that preach the gospel should live by the gospel.[33] "If we have sown unto you spiritual things, is it a great thing if we shall reap your carnal things?"[34] They should minister to them cheerfully with all readiness of mind. Ministers are not to ask for

[29] Heb. 13:5, 17
[30] Jer. 20:10, Zeph. 2:8, 2 Cor. 11:21, 23
[31] Gal. 6:6
[32] 1 Cor. 9:7-8
[33] 1 Cor. 9:14
[34] 1 Cor. 9:11

their bread, but to receive it honorably.[35] The minister's maintenance, though it is not by tithes as under the law, yet they have now as just a right to a comfortable maintenance as they had then. The equity of the duty is the same: "Our Savior," said Dr. Owen, "and the Apostles plead it from grounds of equity and justice; and all kind of laws and rules of righteousness among men of all sorts call for it."[36]

7. It is their duty to adhere to them, and abide by them in all their trials and persecutions for the Word. "Ye were not ashamed of me in my bonds, etc."[37]

8. Dr. Owen adds another duty of the members to their pastor,[38] namely to agree to come together upon his appointment: "When they were come, and had gathered the church together" etc.[39]

[35] Matt. 10:9-10
[36] See Dr. Owen's *Ephod*, 21-22
[37] 2 Tim. 4:16-18
[38] *Ephod*, p. 27.
[39] Acts 14:27

Some Principles on Eldership

Are there not ruling elders besides the pastor?

There might be such in the primitive Apostolic Church, but we see no ground to believe it an abiding office to continue in the church, but was only temporary.

1. Because we have none of the qualifications of such elders mentioned, or how to be chosen.

2. Because we read not particularly what their work and business is, or how distinct from preaching elders. Though we see not, but the church may (if she sees meet) choose some able and discreet brethren to be *helps in government*.[40] We have the qualifications of bishops and deacons directly laid down,[41] and how to be chosen, and their work declared,[42] but of no other office or officers in the church, but these only.

Question

May an elder of one church if called, warrantably administer all ordinances to another?

[40] Rom. 12:8
[41] 1 Tim. 3
[42] Tit. 1:5-7

No surely,[43] for we find no warrant for any such practice, he being only ordained pastor or elder of that particular church that chose him, and has no right or authority to administer as an elder in any other, where he is not so much as a member.[44]

Question

May a church call out a teacher that is not an ordained elder to administer all ordinances to them?

You may as well ask, *May a church act disorderly?* Why were ministers to be ordained, if others who are not ordained might do all their work? If therefore they have no person fitly qualified for that office, they must look out from abroad for one that is. Yet (as we say) necessity has no law; provided therefore they can't do either, it is better their teacher be called to do it than that the church should be without their food and the church ordinances be neglected.

Let all churches take care to organize themselves, and not through covetousness or neglect of duty to rest incomplete churches, and so under sin. "God is the God of order, and not of confusion, in all the churches of the

43 Acts 20:17, 27-28
44 Tit. 1:5

saints."[45] And how severely did God deal of old with such that meddled with the priests work and office, which were not of the priesthood, nor called by him to administer in holy things!

Reception of Members

What is the order of receiving members into the church, that were not members any where before?

The person must give an account of his faith; and of the work of grace upon his soul before the church;[46] and also a strict enquiry must be made about his life and conversation.[47] If through bashfulness the party cannot speak before the congregation,[48] the elder and two or three more persons may receive an account of his or her faith[49] and report it to the church.[50] But if full satisfaction by the testimony of good and credible persons is not given of the party's life and conversation, he must be put by until satisfaction is obtained in that respect.[51]

[45] 1 Cor. 14:33, 38
[46] Ps. 66:16, Acts 9:26-27
[47] 3 John 9:10
[48] Rom. 14:17, 19, 1 Pet. 3.15
[49] 1 Cor. 14:40
[50] Rom. 15:1-2
[51] Acts 11:2-6

Moreover, when the majority is satisfied, and yet one or two persons are not, the church and elders will do well to wait a little time and endeavor to satisfy such persons, especially if the reasons of their difference seem weighty.

Question

What is to be done when a person offers himself for communion from a church that is corrupt, or erroneous in principles?

1. The church ought to take an account of his faith in all fundamental points and of the work of grace upon his heart. 2. And if satisfied, then to send also to that corrupt people, to know whether they have any thing or not against his life and conversation: if satisfied in both these respects, the church may receive him.

Question

To whom is its members to join themselves? is it to the elder, or to the church?

They are joined to the whole community of the church, being incorporated as members thereof, and there to abide: though the pastor be removed by death.[52]

---

[52] Acts 2:47, 5:11, 15

2
The Discipline
of the Church

We judge it necessary that one day a month be appointed for discipline. It is not expedient to manage such affairs on the Lord's Day, which should be spent on the public worship of God. Besides, such things may (on the account of discipline) come before the church, which may not be expedient to be heard on the Lord's Day, lest it disturb the spirits of any members and hinder their meditation on the Word that they have newly heard. Though in small congregations, perhaps a day in two or three months may be sufficient.

The power of the keys, or to receive in and shut out of the congregation, is committed unto the church.[1] The political power of Christ, said Dr. Isaac Chauncy, is in the church, whereby it is exercised in the name of Christ,

---

[1] Acts 16:5, 2 Thess. 1:3, 6

having all lawful rule and government within itself; which he thus proves:

1. The church essential is the first subject of the keys.

2. Necessary for the preservation of the church, they must purge themselves from all pernicious members.

3. They have power to organize themselves with officers. Yet, I humbly conceive, I may add, that the concurrence of the presbytery is needful hereunto.

4. If need be that they call an officer from without, or one of another church, they must first admit him a member, that they may ordain their officer from among themselves.

5. They have power to reject a scandalous pastor from office and membership. This power of Christ is exerted as committed to them by the hands of the elder appointed by Christ, the due management whereof is in and with the church to be his care and trust, as a steward, whereof he is accountable to Christ and the church, not lording it over God's heritage.

And that the power of the keys is in the church appears to me from Matthew 18. *If he will not hear the church;* it is not said, if he will not hear the elder, or elders. As also that of the apostle, in directing the church to cast out the incestuous person;[2] he does not give this counsel to the elder or elders of the church, but to the church.[3] In the same way, he commands the church to withdraw from every brother that walks disorderly. "Purge out the old leaven, that you may be a new lump."[4]

Now as to church-censures I understand but two besides suspension: (1.) withdrawing from a member that walks disorderly and (2.) casting out (or excommunicating) such that are either guilty of notorious or scandalous crimes of heresy, etc. or of contemning the authority of the church.

Briefly to each of these.

1. Suspension is to be when a member falls under sin; and the church wants time fully to hear the matter, and so can't withdraw from him, or cast him out.

2. If any member walks disorderly, though not guilty of gross scandalous sins, he or she, as soon as it is taken notice of, ought to be admonished and the church is to endeavor to be used to bring him to repentance. "For we hear that there are some which walk disorderly, not

[2] 1 Cor. 5:4-5
[3] 2 Thess. 3:6, 14
[4] 1 Cor. 5:7

working at all, but are busy-bodies."[5] Such as meddle with matters that do not concern them, it may be (instead of following their own trade and business) they go about from one member's house to another telling or carrying tales and stories of this brother or of that brother, or sister: which perhaps may be true or perhaps false, and may be also to the reproach or scandal of some member or members; which, if so, it is backbiting. This is so notorious a crime that without repentance they shall not ascend God's holy hill.[6]

Back-biting is a diminishing of our neighbor's or brother's good name, either by denying him his due praise, or by laying anything to his charge falsely, irregularly, or without sufficient cause or evidence. But this of disorderly-walking does not amount to such a crime [*that requires excommunication*],[7] but evils not so notorious; "Now them that are such, we command and exhort by our Lord Jesus Christ, that with quietness they work, and eat their own bread."[8] They must be admonished.

---

[5] 2 Thess. 3:11-12
[6] Ps. 15:1, 3
[7] Words in bracked added by publisher.
[8] 2 Thess. 3:12

A True Admonition

First, an admonition is a faithful endeavor to convict a person of a fault, both as to matter of fact and circumstance. This admonition must be given first, if it be private, by that brother that knows or has knowledge of the fault or evil of the person offending—whether the elder, or member—for any private brother ought to admonish such with all care and faithfulness before he proceeds farther. But if it is a public matter, the church ought to send for the offender, and the pastor must admonish him before all.

Second, if after all due endeavors used he is not reclaimed, but continues a disorderly person, the church must withdraw from him. "Now we command you brethren, in the name of our Lord Jesus Christ, that you withdraw from every brother that walks disorderly, and not after the traditions he received from us."[9] This is not a delivering up to Satan (excommunicating or dismembering the person), for this sort are still to be owned as members, though disorderly ones. The church must note him so as not to have communion or company with him in that sense, "yet count him not as an enemy,

[9] 2 Thess. 2:6

but exhort him as a brother: if any man obey not our word, note that man."[10]

It appears that such who refuse to adhere to what the pastor commands and exhorts to,[11] in the name of Christ, are to be deemed disorderly persons. They are such who meet not with the church when assembled together to worship God, or that neglect private or family prayer, or neglect their attendance on the Lord's Supper, or to contribute to the necessary charges of the church, or suffer any evils unreproved in their children. All such may be looked upon as disorderly-walkers and ought to be proceeded against according to this rule, or divulge the private resolves of the church, as well as in many like cases.

Private Offenses of One Brother against Another

As touching private offenses, the rule *Matthew 18* is to be observed. Only this by the way must be premised: if but one brother or two have the knowledge of some member's crime; yet if it be publicly known to the world, and the name of God be reproached, it being an immoral

[10] 2 Thess. 2:14-15
[11] Heb. 12:25

act, a private brother is not to proceed with such an offender (according to *Matthew 18*) but forthwith to bring it to the church that the public scandal may be taken off.

But if it be a private offense or injury done to a brother or sister in particular, and not being a notorious scandalous sin, that brother must not mention it to one soul, either within, or without the church, until he has proceeded according to the rule.

1. He must tell his brother his fault. "Moreover, if your brother shall trespass against you, go and tell him his fault between you and him alone; if he shall hear you, you have gained your brother."[12] You must labor in love and all affections to convince him of his fault; but if he will not hear you,

2. You must take one or two more, but be sure to see they are discreet persons, and such that are most likely to gain upon him. They with you are to labor with all wisdom to bring him to the sense of his fault. It is not just to speak to him, as if that were enough; no, no, but to take all due pains to strive to convince him so that the matter may be issued and the church not troubled with it. "But if he will not hear you, take one or two more, that in

[12] Matt. 18:15

the mouth of two or three witnesses every word may be established."[13]

3. But if he will not hear them after all due means and admonitions are used, then it must be brought to the church. And if he will not hear the church, he must be cast out. The elder is to put the question whether the offending brother is, in their judgments, incorrigible (refusing to hear the church). Passing in the affirmative by the vote of the congregation, or the majority of the brethren by the lifting up of their hands, or by their silence, the pastor after calling upon God and opening the nature of the offense and the justness of their proceedings, in the name and by the authority of Christ, is to pronounce the sentence of excommunication.

That A.B. being guilty of great iniquity, and not manifesting unfeigned repentance, but refusing to hear the Church, I do in the name, and by the authority of Christ committed unto me as pastor of this his church, pronounce and declare that he is to be, and is hereby excommunicated, excluded, or cast out of the congregation; and no longer to be owned a brother, or a member of this church; and this for the destruction of the flesh, that his spirit may be saved in the day of the Lord Jesus.[14]

---

[13] Matt. 18:16
[14] 1 Cor. 5

And this we believe is the substance of that which the Apostle calls "a delivering up to Satan," he being cast into the world—which is called the kingdom of Satan.

"The delivery unto Satan," claimed Dr. Chauncy, "signifies only the solemn exclusion of a person from the communion of the church, the visible kingdom of Christ, and disenfranchising him, or divesting him of all visible right to church privileges, casting him into the kingdom of the world, where the prince of darkness rules in the children of disobedience." And this being done, he is to be esteemed to be no better than a heathen man, a publican, or as an evil person, and not to have so much as intimate civil communion withal.[15]

Scandalous Persons Guilty of Gross Acts of Immorality

If any member fall into any gross acts of sin, as *swearing, lying, drunkenness, fornication, covetousness, extortion*, or the like, and it is known and publicly spread abroad to the great scandal and reproach of religion, and of the holy name of God, his church, and people, then the church must send one or two brethren to him (the said offender so charged) to come before the congregation. If he will not come, but

[15] Matt. 18:17

does fight and contemn the authority of the church, then this will bring farther guilt upon him, for which offense he incurs the censure before-mentioned.

But if he does appear, his charge is to be laid before him and the witnesses called. After he has made his defense, and said all he has to say, and the congregation finds him guilty, then the same censure is to pass upon him: to the end he may be brought to unfeigned repentance, and the name of God cleared. Some time must be taken to make it appear that he has true repentance—by the reformation of his life and holy walking afterwards—before he is received again, and the censure of the church in a solemn manner be taken off.

Dr. Chauncy puts this Question, '*How is a church to proceed in case of open and notorious scandals?*'

The answer is, the matter of fact, as such, being beyond all question; the church is to proceed immediately to censure, to vindicate the honor of Christ and his church, and to manifest to the world their just indignation against such notorious offenders; and wait for a well-grounded and tried evidence of his true repentance under that ordinance of Christ which is appointed to that end.[16]

---

[16] 1 Tim. 5:24. Acts 5.11. Jude 23, 1 Cor. 5, 2 Cor. 7:11

It is the opinion of the doctor, that though the person be penitent, yet because his sin is open and scandalous, he ought to be cast out to vindicate the honor of Christ and the church, as part of his just punishment (that being one reason of the ordinance of excommunication) as well as to bring the person to thorough repentance; and we are of his mind. Paul takes no notice in the case of the *incestuous person* of his immediate repentance; or if he repent not, then, etc. but says he, *"deliver such a one to Satan..."* The Lord says, "if her father had but spit in her face, should she not be ashamed seven days? Let her be shut out from the camp seven days: (speaking of Miriam) and after that let her be received in again."[17]

Dealing with Heretics and Blasphemers

As touching heretics or heresy, the same censure, when they are convicted, ought to pass against them. Heresy is commonly restrained to signify any perverse opinion or error in a fundamental point of religion, as to deny: the being of God, or the deity of Christ, or his satisfaction, and justification alone by his righteousness, or to deny the resurrection of the body, or eternal judgment, or the like. Yet our annotators say, the word signifies the same thing

---

[17] Num. 12:14

with schism and divisions; which if so, such that are guilty of schism or divisions in the church ought to be excommunicated also.[18] *Heresies* are called *damnable* by the Apostle Peter: without repentance such cannot be saved; "as bring in damnable heresies, denying the Lord that bought them."[19]

Two things render a man a heretic according to the common signification of the word. (1.) An error in matters of faith, fundamental or essential to salvation. (2.) Stubbornness and contumacy in holding and maintaining it. "A man that is an heretic, after the first and second admonition reject."[20]

This rejection is the same as excommunication, as it appears by what Paul speaks, "Of whom is Hymaeneus and Alexander, whom I have delivered unto Satan, that they may learn not to blaspheme."[21] Their heresy or blasphemy was in saying the resurrection was past.

Some would have none be counted an heretic but he who is convicted and condemned so to be in his own conscience, mistaking Paul's words: "Knowing that he

[18] See Pool's *Annot.* on 1 Cor. 11:19
[19] 2 Pet. 2:1
[20] Tit. 3:10
[21] 1 Tim. 1:19-20

that is such, is subverted, being condemned of himself." He may be condemned of himself, though not for his *heresy*, yet for his spending his time about questions, and strife of words to the disquieting the peace of the church; or though not condemned of himself directly, yet indirectly; according to the purport of his own notion, or what he grants about the point in debate, etc. else the apostle refers to some notable and notorious self-condemned heretic.

It is a great question, whether Hymaeneus and Alexander were condemned in their own consciences, about that heresy charged upon them, and yet were delivered up to Satan. However the rule is plain, respecting any that are subverted and resolutely maintain any heretical notion (i.e., after he has been twice admonished, that is, after all due means used, and pains taken with him, to convince him of his abominable error; and yet if he remains obstinate), he must *be delivered up to Satan*. That is, the righteous censure of the church must pass upon him, as in the case of other notorious crimes. Heresy is a work of the flesh: and hence some conceive such ought to be punished by the civil magistrate.

Discipline Particulars

It is a faithful endeavor to convict a person of a fault both as to matter of fact, and his duty thereupon: charging it on his conscience in the name of the Lord Jesus with all wisdom and authority.

Question

What is a church admonition?

When an offending brother rejecting private admonition by one, or by two or three persons, the complaint being brought to the church by the elder, the offending member is rebuked and exhorted in the name of the Lord Jesus to due repentance; and if convicted, and he repents, the church forgives him, otherwise casts him out, as I before showed.

Question

May a church admit a member of another congregation to have communion with them, without an orderly receiving him as a member?

If the person is well known by the church of whom he is visiting, and that he is an orderly member of a church of the same faith, he being occasionally cast among them, then they may admit him to transient communion for that time. If, however, he lives in a town or city that is remote to the church to whom he belongs, he ought to have his regular dismission, and so be delivered up to the care and watch of the church where he abides.

Question

If an excommunicated person has obtained of God true repentance, and desires to be restored to the church; what is the manner of his reception?

Upon his serious, solemn, and public acknowledgment thereof before the church, and due satisfaction according to the nature of his offense being given, the elder solemnly proceeds and declares in the name of the Lord Jesus,[22] that the sentence which *A.B.* was laid under (upon his unfeigned repentance) is taken off,[23] and that he is received again as a member, etc. to the praise and glory of God.[24]

[22] Matt. 13:18
[23] 2 Cor. 2:6-7
[24] 1 Tim. 5

Question

How ought a pastor to be dealt withal, if he to the knowledge of the church, or any members thereof, walks disorderly, and unworthily of his sacred office, and membership?

Take the answer of another author here: "Those members, to whom this is manifestly known, ought to go to him privately, and unknown to any others, (and with the *spirit of meekness, in great humility*) lay his evil before him, and entreat him as a father, and not rebuke him as their equal, much less as their inferior; and if they gain upon him, then to receive him into their former affection and esteem, for ever hiding it from all others. But if after all tender entreaties, he prove refractory and obstinate, then to bring him before the church, and there to deal with him; they having two or three witnesses in the face of the church, to testify matter-of-factly against him to their personal knowledge." But before he be dealt with they must appoint one from among themselves, qualified for the work of a pastor, to execute the church's censure against him, etc. Yet, no doubt, the church may suspend him from his communion, and the exercising of his office presently, upon his being fully convicted. But seeing in the multitude of counsel there is safety, sure no church would so proceed without the advice of the *presbytery*, or of a sister-church at least.

Question

Suppose a member should think himself oppressed by the church; or should be unjustly dealt with; either withdrawn from, or excommunicated, has he no relief left him?

We believe he has relief; and also, that there is no church infallible, but may err in some points of faith, as well as in discipline. And the way proposed and agreed to, in a general assembly held in *London* (1692), of the *elders, ministers, and messengers* of our *churches*, we approve of, which is this:

> The grieved or injured person may make his application to a sister-church for communion; and that church may send some brethren in their names, to that congregation that have dealt with him, and they to see if they can possibly restore him to his place; but if they cannot, then to report the matter charged, with the proofs, to the church that sent them: and if that congregation shall, after a full information, etc. be persuaded the person was not orderly dealt with, they may receive him into their communion.

Those Who Would Leave a Church

Of such that cause divisions, or unduly separate themselves from the church: this I find is generally asserted by all congregational divines, or worthy men (*i.e.,* that no person has power to dismember himself). He cannot, without great sin, translate himself from one church to another; but ought to have a dismission from that church where he is a member; [25] provided that church is orderly constituted, nothing being wanting as to any essential of salvation, or of church communion; but if not, yet he ought to endeavor to get his orderly dismission. Nor is every small difference in some points of religion (or notions of little moment) any grounds for him to desire his dismission.

That he cannot, nor ought not to translate himself, see what a reverend Chauncy said:[26] he cannot, *said he*, for many reasons:

1. It is not decent, much less an orderly going away; but very unmannerly, and a kind of running away.

2. Such a departure is not approved of in families, or civil societies.[27]

3. It destroys the relation of pastor and people: for what may be done by one individual person, may be done by all.

[25] Rom. 6:17
[26] Dr. Chauncy, p. 339.
[27] Phil. 1:27, Tit. 2:10

4. What liberty in this kind belongs to the *sheep*, belongs to the *shepherd*; much more he may then also leave his *flock* at his pleasure, without giving notice or reason thereof to the church.

5. It is breaking *covenant* with Christ, and with the *congregation*, and therefore a great immorality;[28] he being under obligation to abide steadfastly with the church (i.e., till the church judge he has a lawful *call* to go to another congregation).

6. It's a *schism*: for if there be any such thing in the world, it's of particular societies.

7. It is a despising of the government of the church.[29]

8. It is a particular member's assuming to himself thence of the keys; or rather stealing of them.[30]

9. There is as much reason persons should come into a church when they please, with out asking consent, as depart when they please.

10. It is very evil and unkind of another *church* to receive such a one, as *not doing as they would, or should be dealt with.*

[28] Rom. 1:31
[29] Acts 2:42, 1 Cor. 12:6, 14, 7:5
[30] Heb. 10:25

11. Such practices can issue in nothing else than the *breach* and *confusion* of all particular *churches*; and make them like *parishes*.

12. Such departures cannot be pleaded for in the least, but upon the notion of a *catholic* visible church, wherein all members and officers are run into one *organized church*, which will, and must introduce, a coordinate (if not a *subordinate*) pastoral government, by combination of *elders*, over all the churches; and therefore by *synods* and *classes*.

13. It is like a leak in a ship, which, if not speedily stopped, will sink at last.

14. It tends to anarchy: putting an *arbitrary power* in every member.

15. It breaks all bonds of love, and raises the greatest animosities between brethren and churches.

16. It is a great argument of some guilt lying on the party. Thus the doctor again said, It is no more in the just power of a particular member to dissolve his church-relation, than in a man to kill himself: but by his said withdrawal he does schismatically rend himself from his communion, and so separate himself sinfully.[31]

---

[31] Jude 19, 1 Cor. 1:10, 3:3, 11:18, Heb. 10:22-25

Question

What is the just act of the church, that clothes this irregular separation, with the formality as it were of an excommunication?

He answers by calling this a mixed excommunication (*i.e.*, originally proceeding from, and consists in, the act of the brother himself, and is the formality of his offense; upon which proceeds the just and inviolable act of the church).

The judgment of the church publicly declared by the elder of the congregation; as the doctor words it: *That A.B. having so and so irregularly and sinfully withdrawn himself from the communion of the congregation, we do now adjudge him a non-member, and one that is not to communicate with the church,*[32] *in the special ordinances of communion, until due satisfaction is given by him.*[33]

Yet we believe, as the doctor's opinion is that a church may (if they find the case to be warranted by the word of God; or as it may be circumstanced) give a dismission to a member, when insisted on, to another regular church: though not in every case of small offense, or dissent in some small points of different notions, or from prejudice;

[32] Rom. 9:17-18, 2 Thess. 3:6, 14-15
[33] Jude 12

for that may tend soon to dissolve any *church*. For what church is it, where every member is of one mind in every particular case and thing about notions of religion?

And such that make divisions, and cause schisms—or discord among brethren—to disturb the peace of the *church*:[34] if they cannot be reclaimed, must be marked[35] and dealt with as great *offenders*;[36] it being one of those things that God hates, and is an abomination to him.

Question

What is a full and lawful dismission of a member to another church, upon his removing his habitation, or on other warranted cases?

We answer, a letter, testimonial, or recommendation of the person; and if he intends to abide there wholly, to give him up to that *communion* and *fellowship*,[37] to be watched over in the Lord.

[34] 2 Tim. 2:23
[35] 2 Thess. 3:14
[36] Pro. 6.16
[37] Rom. 16:1-2

3
Common Causes
of Discord

1. One cause of discord is through the ignorance in some members of the rules of discipline and right government:[1] particularly when that rule in Matthew 18 is not followed.

But one person takes up an offense against another, and speaks of it to this or that person, before he has told the brother offending of it; which is a palpable sin, and a direct violation of Christ's holy precept: and such must, as offenders themselves, be in a gospel-way dealt with.

To prevent this, the discipline of the church should be taught; and the members informed of their duties.

2. Another thing that causes trouble and disorder in a church is a lack of love and tender affections toward one another; as also not having a full sight and sense of the

---

[1] Matt. 18:15

great evil of breaking the bonds of *peace and unity*.[2] O that all would lay this abominable *evil* to heart! How base a thing it is to break the peace of a private family, or neighborhood:[3] but much more sinful to disturb the peace of the church of the living God, and break the bonds of the unity thereof. "Behold, how good, and how pleasant it is, for brethren to dwell together in unity!"[4] But, O how ugly and hateful is the contrary!

3. Another disorderly practice is this: when one member or another knows of some sinful act or evils done by one or more members, and they conceal it;[5] or do not act according to the rule—pretending they would not be looked upon as contentious persons.[6] However, hereby they may become guilty of other men's sins, and also suffer the name of God and the church to lie under reproach, and all through their neglect. This is a great iniquity.

4. When an elder or church knows that some persons are scandalous in their lives or heretical in judgment, and yet shall bear or connive with them.

---

[2] John 13:12, 17. Eph. 4:3
[3] Heb. 13:1, Eph. 4:31-32, Eph. 5:2
[4] Ps. 132:1, Jam. 3:16
[5] Acts 5:3, 8
[6] Lev. 19:17

5. When members take liberty to hear at other places, when the church is assembled to worship God:[7] this is nothing less than a breaking their covenant with the church, and may soon dissolve any church: for by the same rule, one may take that liberty, another; nay, every member may. Moreover, it casts a contempt upon the ministry of the church, and tends to cause such who are hearers to draw off and to be disaffected with the doctrine taught in the church, (they knowing these dissenters do belong unto it).

I exhort, therefore, in the name of Christ, that this may be prevented. And any of you that know who they are that take this liberty: pray discover them to the church. We lay no restraint upon our members from hearing such, who are found in the faith at other times.

6. The liberty that some take to hear men that are corrupt in their judgments; and so take in unsound notions, and also strive to distill them into the minds of others, as if they were of great importance. Alas, how many are corrupted in these days with *arminianism, socinianism,* and what not. This causes great trouble and disorder.

[7] Acts 4:23

7. When one church shall receive a member or members of another congregation without their consent or knowledge: nay such that are disorderly and may be loose-livers, or cast out for immorality, or persons filled with prejudice without cause. This is enough to make men atheists, or contemn all church authority and religion: for has not one regular church as great authority from Christ as another.[8]

8. Another disorder is when members are received without the general consent of the church;[9] or before good satisfaction is taken of their godly lives and conversations. Or when a church is too remiss in the reception of her members.

9. Another disorder is when a church shall receive a charge against a member (it being an offense between brother and brother) before an orderly proceeding has been made by the offended person.[10]

10. When judgment passes with partiality; some are connived at out of favor or affection. *Levi* was not to know his *father* or *mother* in judgment.

[8] 2 Pet. 2:2
[9] Acts 9:27
[10] Matt. 18:15

11. When members do not constantly and early attend our public assemblies,[11] and the worship of God on the Lord's day especially,[12] but are remiss in that matter; this is a great evil.[13]

12. When part of a church shall meet together as dissatisfied to consult church-matters, without the knowledge or consent of the church or pastor. This is disorderly, and tends to division; and such should be marked.[14]

13. Another thing that tends to disquiet the peace of the church is when there are any undue heat of spirit, or passion shown in the pastor, or others, in managing the discipline of the church. Have we not found by experience the sad effect of this? Therefore things must be always managed with coolness, sweetness of spirit, and moderation; every brother having liberty to speak his mind and not to be interrupted until he has done; nor above one speak at once.[15]

[11] Ps. 63:1
[12] Cant. 7:12
[13] Mark 15:1
[14] 1 Cor. 13:25, Rom. 16:17
[15] 2 Tim. 2:25

14. When one brother or more dissents in the sentiments of their minds from the church in any matters circumstantial; either in respect of faith, practice, or discipline, and will not submit to the majority, but raise feuds;[16] nay, will rend themselves from the church, rather than consent.[17]

Question

What reason, or ground, has any man to refuse communion with a church that Christ has not left, but has communion with?

15. When any member shall divulge, or make known to persons not of the congregation, nor being concerned in those matters, what is done in church meetings. The church in this respect (as well as in others) is to be as "a garden enclosed, a spring shut up, a fountain sealed."[18] This oft times occasions great grief; and the disorderly person should be detected. Is it not a shame to any of a private family, to divulge the secrets of the family? But far greater shame do these expose themselves unto.

[16] Jude 19
[17] Jam. 3:14, 16
[18] Cant. 4:12

16. Another disorderly practice is this: when a member shall suggest, and seem to insinuate into the minds of other members some evil against their pastor, yet will not declare what it is; and may only be evil surmisings, and out of prejudice; and yet refuses to acquaint the pastor with what it is.[19] This is very abominable, and a palpable violation of the rule of the gospel, and duty of members to their minister. Such a person ought to be severely rebuked; and if he confess not his evils, and manifest unfeigned repentance, to be dealt with farther.

Moreover, it is a great evil in another to hear such base insinuations, and neither rebuke the accuser—and so discharge his duty—or take two or three more to bring the person to repentance. If he deal thus by a private brother it is a great evil, but far worse to an *elder*, whose name and honor ought with all care and justice to be kept up as being more sacred.[20]

17. Another disorderly practice is (which causes much trouble) when the public charges of a church are not equally born but some too much burdened, when others do but little or nothing.[21]

---

[19] Rom. 1:29, 1 Tim. 6:4, Zech. 7:10, 1 Tim. 5:19
[20] 1 Tim. 5:19
[21] 1 Cor. 8:14

And also, when every one does not contribute to the poor, as God has blessed them, on every Lord's Day, or first day of the week, as he has commanded.

18. Another disorder is this: when members refuse to communicate with the church at the Lord's Table, because some person or persons they think are guilty of evil, and yet they have not proceeded with them according to rule.[22] These either excommunicate the church or themselves, or at least those persons that they censure unwarrantably. I beseech you for Christ's sake, that this may never be any more among you. You ought not to deal thus with them or refuse your communion (though faulty) until the church has dismembered or withdrawn from them; or at least suspended them.

19. When one member shall believe, or receive a report against another, before he knows the truth of the matter.[23]

20. When an accusation is brought against an *elder*, contrary to the rule, which ought not be without two or three witnesses, as to the matter of fact.[24]

[22] Matt. 18.
[23] Jer. 20:10
[24] 1 Tim. 5:19

21. When the Word of God is not carefully attended upon on week or lecture days by the members generally, when the said meetings are appointed by the whole church.

22. When days of prayer and fasting, and of public thanksgiving, or when days of disciplining are not generally attended upon.[25]

23. When gifted brethren are not duly encouraged, first privately to exercise their gifts; and being in time approved, called forth to preach or exercise in the church. And when encouragement is not given to bestow learning also upon them, for their better accomplishment. What will become of the churches in time to come, if this be not prevented with speed?

[25] Joel 2:16

4
The Beauty
of a True Church

That which primarily tends to the glory of a church is the foundation on which it is built, which is Jesus Christ. Now this is a blessed and glorious foundation:[1]

The Church's Foundation

In respect of God the Father, who laid this foundation in his eternal purpose, counsel, and decree: *Behold I lay in Zion.*[2] This is as the result of his infinite wisdom, love, and mercy to his elect.

In respect had unto Christ himself, who is this foundation. Christ is a suitable foundation for four reasons. (1.) Christ is a suitable foundation for the church in respect to the glory of God in all his attributes. (2.)

[1] 1 Cor. 3:4
[2] Isa. 28:16

Christ is a suitable foundation in respect to our good: the answering all our wants, who are united to him, or built upon him. (3.) Christ is a suitable foundation in respect of his preciousness: a *precious stone*. (4.) Christ is a suitable foundation in respect to the durableness of it (*i.e., as a tried stone*; a sure foundation).[3]

Brethren, of necessity a foundation of a house must be laid. No house can be built without a good foundation that will stand firm and unmovable. It is the strongest part of the building, for it bears all the weight of the whole superstructure: so does Jesus Christ.

The Church's Constitution

The beauty and glory of a true *church* consists in the true and regular, or right *constitution* of it; nothing being wanting that is essential to it, upon this account.

The Church's Materials

It consists in the excellency, glory, and suitableness of the materials it is built with, answering to the foundation, *all precious stones, lively stones; all regenerated persons.*[4]

---

[3] Isa. 28:16
[4] 1 Pet. 2:5-6

In that all the stones are well hewn and squared; all made fit for the building, before laid in. Were it thus, there would not be so great a noise of the hammer and ax in church discipline, as indeed there is. It was not thus in the type, I mean in *Solomon's Temple*.[5]

It's beauty and glory consists in that all the *stones* being not only united by the Spirit to *Christ*, the foundation, but also to one another in sincere love and affection. "In whom all the building, fitly framed together, grows up unto an holy temple in the Lord."[6]

The Church's Character

It consists in the holiness and purity of the lives and conversations of all the members: "Be *Holy*, for I am Holy."[7] "*Holiness* becomes your house, O God, forever."[8]

It consists in the sweet union and concord that ought to be in the church; all like the horses in Pharaoh's chariot, drawing together:[9] "Endeavoring to keep the unity of the Spirit in the bond of peace."[10] "By this shall

5 1 Kings 6:7
6 Eph. 2:19-21
7 1 Pet. 1:16
8 Ps. 93:5
9 Cant. 1:9
10 Eph. 4:3

all men know you are my disciples, if you love one
another."[11]

The church is beautiful in their having the divine
presence with them; or when the glory of God fills his
temple.[12]

In keeping out all unsanctified, or unclean persons; or
if they get in, to purge them out by a strict and holy
discipline, or else it will soon lose its beauty.[13]

In that zeal and equality that should be shown in all to
keep up the honor, peace, and comfort of the *church* and
the ministry thereof.[14]

The Church's Administration

In the administration of right discipline: to see neither
neglect nor delaying of justice, through carelessness or
partiality: (1.) No ways partaking of other men's sins;
which may be done by conniving at it. (2.) By the
lessening or extenuating of it. (3.) By countenancing, or
any ways encouraging any in sin. (4.) By not restoring a

[11] John 13:35
[12] Ex. 20:24, Matt. 18:20
[13] 1 Cor. 5:5-7
[14] 2 Cor. 8:14, Tit. 3:2

brother, that confesses his sin when overtaken. (5.) Not bringing in a just charge against an offender, nor rebuking him; and yet have communion with him. (6.) Not to wrest judgment out of it's true and right channel, nor to inflict a greater censure than the law of Christ requires on any. (7.) Timely to acquit, and discharge a penitent person. (8.) Not to do any thing out of prejudice, but in love, and bowels of affection; and to do all in Christ's name, or by his authority.

To *sympathize* with the *afflicted, succour* the *tempted,* and *relieving* the *poor* and *distressed; rejoicing* with them that *rejoice,* and *mourning* with them that *mourn.*

To speak evil of no man; not only speaking no evil of their brethren, but of no *man,* to his hurt or injury, detracting from his worth and honor; see *Sirach, Whether it be to friend or foe, talk not of other men's lives; and if you can, without offense, reveal them not.*[15] We must not discourse his faults, unless in a gospel-way; and that too, to amend the person, and not out of passion or prejudice to expose him—but out of love to his soul. Yet, we may speak of the evils of others, (1.) when called to do it, in a legal or gospel way; and it is a sin then to conceal his crime; (2.) Or when it is to prevent

[15] Ecc. 19:8

another, who is in danger to be infected by his company or ill example; (3.) Or in our own just defense and vindication. Moreover, consider the evil of reproaching of others.

Causes of Speaking Evil of Others

1. One cause is from want of love, nay from malice and hatred.

2. Another cause is from the baseness, ill nature, and cruelty of the accuser's *disposition*.

3. It is occasioned from that itch of talking and meddling in the *affairs* of other men.

4. Or perhaps to raise their own esteem and honor, some *degrade* their brother—which is *abominable*. Consider: it is *theft* or *robbery*; nay, and it is worse than to rob a man of his goods, because you take away that which perhaps you cannot restore again. Moreover, consider that such who reproach others, lay themselves open thereby to reproach.

5. Know that he that receives, or hearkens to the scandal is as guilty as the *accuser*; he is like a person that receives stolen goods, and so is as bad as the thief.

This being one of the grand and notorious evils of these *days* I speak the more to it. If you abominate this evil, and avoid it, you will shine in *grace* and *virtue* the more clearly.

Alas, in our days, some that would be thought to be great professors stick not to vilify Christ's ministers, even some of the best of men; and are so full of malice, they care not what wrong they do to their brethren, nor to the truth itself or interest of God. And so, expose themselves to a lasting shame, and their spirit and practice to an abhorrence;[16] they are like cursed *Ham* who discovered his father;[17] these persons violate all laws, both human and Divine.

Motives to Bearing Each Other's Burdens

When they bear one another's burdens, *and so fulfill the law of Christ*,[18] and that you may do this: consider where is that church in which there are no burdens to be borne?

[16] 3 John 9, 10
[17] Gen. 9:22
[18] Gal. 6:2

1. Consider what a burden Jesus Christ has borne for you.

2. What a burden you have to bear of your own.[19]

3. Are you not in some things a burden to the brethren?

4. Do you not desire others to help you bear your burdens?

5. May not God cause you to bear a more heavy burden: because you cannot bear your brother's?

6. It is fulfilling the law of love, nay the *law* of Christ.[20]

The Church's Authority and Offices

The glory and beauty of a congregation is the more manifest when the authority of the church, and the dignity of the pastoral office is maintained. How great was the *evil of the gain-saying of Korah?*[21] The Apostle speaks of some that are "self-willed and presumptuous, who are not afraid to speak evil of dignities."[22]

---

[19] 2 Cor. 7:9
[20] Rom. 3:10
[21] Num. 22:7, 21, Jude 11
[22] 2 Pet. 2:10

God has put a glory and high dignity upon the church and in it's authority and power: *Whom you bind on earth, shall be bound in heaven.*

Moreover, the pastoral office is an office of dignity; they are called *rulers, angels, fathers.* [23] For any therefore to cast contempt on the church or pastor is a great evil, and a reproach to Christ; and tends to disorder and confusion.[24]

The beauty is clearly seen when holiness, righteousness, charity, humility, and all true piety is pressed upon the consciences of every member, and appears in the minister; also that all strive to excel therein, with their uttermost care and diligences.[25]

[23] Rev. 2:1
[24] 1 Tim. 3:5, Acts 23:5
[25] Ps. 110:3, 1 Pet. 1:25

The Membership
of the Church

Know my brethren, *"that God loves the gates of Zion more than all the dwelling places of Jacob."* [1] Therefore, the public worship of God ought to be preferred before private.

(1.) This supposes there must be a visible church. (2.) And it supposes that the church frequently meets together to worship God. (3.) That they have an orderly ministry and at least one ordained *elder* to administer all public ordinances. (4.) Moreover, that all persons have free liberty to assemble with the church and to partake of all ordinances, save those which peculiarly belong to the church; as the Lord's Supper, holy discipline, and days of prayer and fasting. Then the church of old separated themselves from all strangers.[2] Yet, others may attend on

---

[1] Ps. 87:2
[2] Neh. 1:2

all other public ordinances with the church; as public prayer, reading, and preaching the Word, and in singing *God's* praises, as has formerly been proved. May others, my brethren, join in prayer with us, and not praise *God* with us?

Motives

But, O my brethren! Let me beseech you to show your high value and estimation for the public worship of God.

1. Since *God* prefers it thus, or has so great esteem of his public worship.

2. Because he is said to dwell in *Zion; It is his habitation for ever.* The place, where his honor dwells.[3]

3. Here God is most glorified. In his *Temple* every one speaks of his glory; "My Praise shall be in the great congregation."[4]

4. Here is most of God's gracious presence (as one observes it). (1.) His effectual presence, in all places; "where I record my name, thither will I come; and there will I bless you."[5] (2.) Here is more of his intimate

[3] Ps. 132:13, Ps. 26:8
[4] Ps. 29:9
[5] Ex. 20:24

presence: "Where two or three are gathered together in my name, there am I in the midst of them."[6] (3.) He walks in the midst of the seven *golden candlesticks.*[7]

5. Here are the clearest manifestations of God's beauty, which made holy *David* desire *to dwell there for ever.*[8]

6. In that it is said, that those that should be saved, in the Apostles days, *God* added unto the Church.[9]

7. Here is most spiritual advantage to be obtained: *Here the dews of Hermon fall, they descend upon the Mountain of Zion. Here God commands the blessing, even life for evermore, I will abundantly bless her Provision, and satisfy her poor with bread.* Here *David's* doubt was resolved.[10]

8. Here you received your first spiritual breath, or life; many souls are daily born to Christ. That good which is most diffusive is to be preferred; but that good which most partake of is most diffusive; "O magnify the Lord with me! Let us exalt his name together."[11] Live coals separated, soon die.

---

[6] Matt. 13:20
[7] Rev. 1:13
[8] Ps. 27:4, See the appearance of Christ to the Churches, *Rev.* 2:3, 6
[9] Acts 2:47
[10] Ps. 132:13, Ps. 130:15, Ps. 73:1. Ps. 87:5
[11] Ps. 34:3

9. Brethren (as a worthy *divine* observes) the church in her public worship is the nearest resemblance of heaven—especially in singing God's praises. What esteem also did God's worthies of old have for God's public worship? "My Soul longs, yea, even faints for the courts of the Lord. How amiable are your tabernacles, O Lord of Hosts!"[12]

10. See how the promises of *God* run to *Zion*, or to his *church*. [13] *He will bless you out of Zion*. O let nothing discourage you in your waiting at the posts of Christ's door.[14] *David desired rather to be a door-keeper in the house of God, than to dwell in the tents of wickedness.*[15]

Yet nevertheless do not neglect, for the Lord's sake, private devotion—secret, and family prayer. O pray to be fitted for public worship! Come out of your closets to the church.[16] What signifies all you do in public, if you are not such that keep up the worship of God in your own families?

---

[12] Ps. 84:1-2
[13] Isa. 35
[14] Ps. 128:3
[15] Ps. 51:3, Pro. 8:34, Ps. 26:14, Ps. 87:4
[16] Matt. 6:6. Jer. 10:25

O neglect not prayer, reading, and meditation! And take care also to educate and catechize your *children*; and live as men and women *that are dead to this world*; and walk for the Lord's sake, as becomes the *gospel*.[17]

See that *zeal* and *knowledge* go together; a good *conversation* and a good *doctrine* go together. These *two* together, are better than *one*.

Brethren, he that makes the Word of God his rule in whatsoever he does, and the glory of God his end in what he does, shall have the Spirit of God to be his strength. This is like *Solomon's* three-fold cord that will be one, or it will be three; it can't be two, nor can it be broken.[18]

[17] Eph. 6:4, Phil. 1:27
[18] Ecc. 4:9-13

The Solemn Covenant

The Solemn Covenant of the Church of Christ,
Meeting in White-street, at its Constitution
June, 5, 1696

We who desire to walk together in the fear of the Lord, do, through the assistance of his Holy Spirit, profess our deep and serious humiliation for all our transgressions. And we do also solemnly, in the presence of God, of each other, in the sense of our own unworthiness, give up ourselves to the Lord, in a church state according to the Apostolical constitution that he may be our God, and we may be his people, through the Everlasting Covenant of his free grace: in which alone we hope to be accepted by him, through his blessed Son Jesus Christ, whom we take to be our High Priest, to justify and sanctify us, and our Prophet to teach us; and to be subject to him as our Law-giver, and the King of saints; and to conform to all his holy laws and ordinances, for our growth, establishment, and consolation; that we may be as a holy spouse unto him, and serve him in our generation, and wait for his second appearance, as our glorious Bridegroom.[1]

[1] Ezek. 16:6-8, 2 Cor. 8:5, Hos. 2:23, 2 Cor. 6:16

Being fully satisfied in the way of church communion, and the truth of grace in some good measure upon one another's spirits, we do solemnly join ourselves together in a holy union and fellowship— humbly submitting to the discipline of the gospel, and all holy duties required of a people in such a spiritual relation.[2]

1. We do promise and engage to walk in all holiness, godliness, humility, and brotherly love, as much as in us lies to render our communion delightful to God, comfortable to ourselves, and lovely to the rest of the Lord's people.[3]

2. We do promise to watch over each other's conversations, and not to suffer sin upon one another, so far as God shall discover it to us, or any of us; and to stir up one another to love and good works: to warn, rebuke, and admonish one another with meekness according to the rules left to us of Christ in that behalf.[4]

3. We do promise in an especial manner to pray for one another, and for the glory and increase of the church, and for the presence of God in it, and the pouring forth of his Spirit on it, and his protection over it to his glory.[5]

[2] Ex. 26:3-6, Isa. 62:5, Ps. 122:3, Eph. 2:23, Eph. 4:16, 1 Pet. 2:5, Ps. 93:5, Isa. 55:8, Luke 1:74-75

[3] 2 Cor. 7:1,1 Tim. 6:10, 2 Pet. 1:6-7, Acts 20:19, Phil. 2:3, John 13:34, John 15:12

[4] 1 Pet. 1:22, Lev. 19:17, Heb. 10:24-25, 1 Thess. 5:14-15, Rom. 1:15

[5] Eph. 6:18, Lam. 5:16, Col. 4:12

4. We do promise to bear one another's burdens, to cleave to one another, and to have a fellow-feeling with one another, in all conditions both outward and inward, as God in his providence shall cast any of us into. [6]

5. We do promise to bear with one another's weakness, failings, and infirmities, with much tenderness, not discovering to any without the church, nor any within, unless according to Christ's rule, and the order of the gospel provided in that case. [7]

6. We do promise to strive together for the truths of the gospel, and purity of God's ways and ordinances: to avoid causes and causers of division, "endeavoring to keep the unity of the Spirit in the bond of peace" (Eph. 4:3). [8]

7. We do promise to meet together on the Lord's Days, and at other times, as the Lord shall give us opportunities; to serve and glorify God in the way of his worship, to edify one another, and to contrive the good of the church. [9]

8. We do promise according to our ability (or as God shall bless us with the good things of this world) to communicate to our pastor or minister, God having ordained that they that preach the gospel should live of the Gospel. (And now can anything lay a greater

[6] Gal. 6:2, Heb. 12:12, Heb. 13:3, Rom. 12:15, 2 Cor. 11:29
[7] 1 John 3:17-18, Gal. 6:1, 1 Thess. 5:14, Rom. 15:12, Eph. 4:31-32
[8] Jude 3, Gal 5:1, Tit. 3:9-10, 3 John 5, 10
[9] Heb. 3:10, Heb. 10:25, Mal. 3:16, Rom. 14:18, Rom. 15:16

obligation upon the conscience than this covenant: what then is the sin of such who violate it?).[10]

These and all other gospel duties we humbly submit unto, promising and purposing to perform, not in our own strength, being conscious of our own weakness, but in the power and strength of the blessed God, whose we are, and whom we desire to serve: To whom be glory now and for evermore. Amen.

[10] 2 Cor. 9:7-13, Gal. 6:6